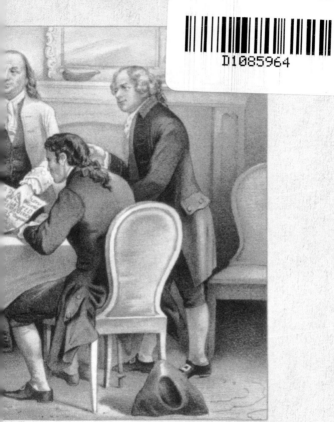

In the Office of the Librarian of Congress at Washington.

135 NASSAU ST. NEW YORK.

FRANKLIN.   ROBERT R. LIVINGSTON.   JOHN ADAMS.

N COMMITTEE.

of Pensylvania, ROGER SHERMAN of Connecticut, ROBERT R. LIVINGSTON of New York.
resolution offered in Congress, June 7ᵗʰ 1776, by Richard Henry Lee, of Virginia.
y upon the Committee,) the Declaration was prepared by the Chairman,
gress July 1ˢᵗ and at mid-day July 4ᵗʰ 1776, the Thirteen Colonies were declared.
of, the United States of America.

THIS BOOK BELONGS TO

_____

BENJAMIN FRANKLIN

NOTEBOOK

CIDER MILL
PRESS

BOOK
PUBLISHERS

Kennebunkport, Maine

Introduction

BY GORDON S. WOOD, AUTHOR OF
THE AMERICANIZATION OF BENJAMIN FRANKLIN AND
THE PULITZER PRIZE-WINNING *THE RADICALISM OF
THE AMERICAN REVOLUTION*

Benjamin Franklin (1706-1790) was certainly the most famous American in the eighteenth-century, known throughout all of North America and Europe. But, even more remarkable, over the past two centuries Franklin emerged to become the most famous figure in American history celebrated throughout the world. His *Autobiography*, which was published only after his death, is the most widely read and translated autobiography in history. The persona he invented in his *Autobiography* has created a powerful posthumous image of Franklin that did not exist in his own lifetime. That image is the Franklin most people know.

Franklin has come to represent America and the American Dream in a way no other person has. Born in the humblest of circumstances—as the youngest son of the seventeen children of a soap and candle maker—Franklin rose through his printing firm and his writings to become one of the wealthiest men in all of North America. Consequently, he has become the model of social mobility and the self-made man—demonstrating the capacity of ordinary people to make it to the top through frugality and hard work. All of the homely Poor Richard maxims of his almanac—"Early to bed and early to rise, makes a man healthy, wealthy, and wise"—have fashioned the image of the middle-class moralist preoccupied with the getting and saving of money.

Early in the twentieth century, the famous German sociologist Max Weber saw in Franklin the perfect representative of the "Protestant ethic" and the modern capitalistic spirit. Because Franklin became the symbol of America's middle-class business values, he also became the object of hostile criticism by imaginative writers, ranging from Edgar Allan Poe, Henry David Thoreau, and Herman Melville to Mark Twain and D.H. Lawrence, who didn't like any celebration of the making of money.

Even without Franklin's extraordinary posthumous image, the reality of his life in the eighteenth century is amazing enough. No one was more inventive and more insatiably curious. He kept notes about everything that puzzled him. What was the relationship between oil and water? How did crabs propagate themselves? Why was it two weeks faster sailing east across the Atlantic than traveling west? What kind of rigging of sails would make a ship steadier? Even when he had no immediate explanation for something, he jotted down notes for future consideration.

Because of his inventions of the lightning rod, bifocals, the Franklin stove, and other useful instruments, he is often seen as a simple inventor, an early version of Thomas Edison. But he made his name in the eighteenth century not simply as an inventor but as a contributor to the fundamentals of science. If there had been a Nobel Prize for physics in the eighteenth century, his discoveries of electricity would have made him a contender. His book on electricity went through five English editions—three in French, one in Italian, and one in German. Those scientific discoveries established his worldwide fame, a fame that was enhanced by the fact that he was an unknown American living in a far-off land that many Europeans regarded as undeveloped, savage, and scarcely capable of enlightened science.

Although Franklin had only two years of formal schooling, he was a voracious reader and taught himself everything, including several foreign languages. He was awarded honorary degrees by nearly all the American colleges and by St. Andrews and Oxford in Britain. Royal academies in Britain and France made him members; in the case of the French Academy, he was one of only eight foreigners so honored. He spent much of his life after age fifty living abroad, where he hobnobbed with every important person, even conversing and dining with kings.

Despite his scientific achievements, however, Franklin always believed that public service was more important than science. He worked tirelessly to create a civic society in Philadelphia, and helped to establish institutions that hadn't existed before in the city and in some cases hadn't existed anywhere in North America—a fire company, an insurance company, a library, and a hospital. He founded the American Philosophical Society and helped reform the postal service of North America. He suggested the ideas of matching grants and daylight saving time, and instituted the practice of franchising by supplying capital to printing businesses up and down the continent of North America in return for a share in the profits.

Among the Founding Fathers, he was second in importance only to George Washington. Franklin was the only one to have a hand in drafting all the great documents of the Revolution. He was

Dost thou love Life?
then do not squander Time;
for that's the Stuff
Life is made of.

—*POOR RICHARD'S ALMANACK* (JUNE 1746)

on the committee that wrote the Declaration of Independence. He was involved in writing both the 1776 state constitution of Pennsylvania and the Articles of Confederation, America's first national constitution. He was a member of the commission that negotiated the peace treaty of 1783 by which Britain recognized the independence of the United States. And in 1787 he was the oldest member of the Philadelphia Convention that created the federal Constitution.

Most important was his contribution as a diplomat in France. Not only did he secure diplomatic recognition for the new republic of the United States, but by dressing in plain clothes at the court of Versailles, the most protocol-ridden court in Europe, and posing as the simple backwoods philosopher, he played upon the French aristocracy's radical-chic infatuation with America, and extracted from an increasingly impoverished French monarchy financial aid that made continuation of the American Revolution possible. Since no other American could have done what he did in France, he can lay claim to being America's most important diplomat.

Beneath all of his massive symbolism, it is clear that Franklin was a truly great man.

Poor Richard, 1743.

A N

Almanack

For the Year of Chriſt

1 7 4 3,

Being the Third after LEAP YEAR.

And makes ſince the Creation	Years
By the Account of the Eaſtern *Greeks*	7251
By the Latin Church, when ⊙ ent. ♈	6942
By the Computation of *W. W.*	5752
By the *Roman* Chronology	5692
By the *Jewiſh* Rabbies	5504

Wherein is contained,

The Lunations, Eclipſes, Judgment of the Weather, Spring Tides, Planets Motions & mutual Aſpects, Sun and Moon's Riſing and Setting, Length of Days, Time of High Water, Fairs, Courts, and obſervable Days.

Fitted to the Latitude of Forty Degrees, and a Meridian of Five Hours Weſt from *London*, but may without ſenſible Error, ſerve all the adjacent Places, even from *Newfoundland* to *South-Carolina*.

By *RICHARD SAUNDERS*, Philom.

PHILADELPHIA:
Printed and ſold by *B. FRANKLIN*, at the New Printing-Office near the Market.

Title page for Poor Richard, 1743, an Almanack.

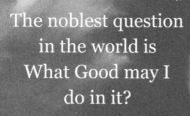

The noblest question
in the world is
What Good may I
do in it?

—*POOR RICHARD'S ALMANACK* (1737)

Half-length portrait of Benjamin Franklin holding the book "Electric Expts," with scientific instruments to his left and a lightning strike in the background. From a painting by Benjamin Wilson, 1761.

Wish

not so much to live long as

to live well.

—*POOR RICHARD'S ALMANACK* (1738)

We must all hang
together,
or most assuredly we shall
all hang separately.

—*AT THE SIGNING OF THE DECLARATION
OF INDEPENDENCE* (1776)

Declaration of Independence *painting, commissioned in 1817,*
showing the document's five-man drafting committee
(which included Franklin). The image is reproduced
on the back of the two-dollar bill.

I grew convinced that

truth, sincerity, and integrity

in dealings between man
and man, were of the

utmost importance to the felicity of life...

—THE AUTOBIOGRAPHY OF BENJAMIN FRANKLIN (1791)

Statue celebrating Franklin as PRINTER, *near the Old Post Office in Washington, D.C.*

Without Freedom of Thought,
there can be no such
Thing as Wisdom;
and no such
Thing as
publick Liberty,
without Freedom of Speech.

—BENJAMIN FRANKLIN, WRITING AS SILENCE DOGOOD,
NO. 8 (JULY 9, 1722)

No gains
without pains.

—POOR RICHARD'S ALMANACK (APRIL 1745)

Benjamin Franklin discussing the Treaty of Paris with the British diplomat Richard Oswald; an illustration in Scribner *Magazine in 1898.*

Sell not virtue
to purchase wealth,
nor Liberty
to purchase power.

—*POOR RICHARD'S ALMANACK* (1738)

Benjamin Franklin conversing with a man and a woman on a boat-flecked river in France, from a print c. 1888.

If you would
be loved,
love and
be loveable.

—POOR RICHARD'S ALMANACK (1755)

If you wish

information and
improvement

from the knowledge of others, and

yet at the same time
express yourself as
firmly fix'd

in your present opinions, modest,
sensible men, who do not love
disputation, will probably leave you
undisturbed in

the possession
of your error.

—*THE AUTOBIOGRAPHY OF BENJAMIN FRANKLIN* (1791)

Haste makes Waste.

—POOR RICHARD'S ALMANACK (JUNE 1753)

Benjamin Franklin reads the Declaration of Independence while John Adams (seated) and Thomas Jefferson look on. From a painting by J.L.G. Ferris, c. 1921.

There never was
a good War or
a bad Peace.

— LETTER TO JOSIAH QUINCY (SEPTEMBER 11, 1783)

Hide not your Talents,

they for Use were made.

What's a Sun-Dial

in the Shade!

—*POOR RICHARD'S ALMANACK* (1750)

*Franklin as editor and writer. Photograph of a painting by
Charles E. Mills, published sometime between 1900 and 1920.*

The ordaining of laws in favor of

one part of the nation, to the prejudice and oppression of another, is certainly the most erroneous and mistaken policy.

An equal dispensation

of protection, rights, privileges, and advantages, is what every part is entitled to, and

ought to enjoy.

—EMBLEMATICAL REPRESENTATIONS, CIRCA 1774

Genius
without Education
is like Silver
in the Mine.

—POOR RICHARD'S ALMANACK (1750)

THE PHILOSOPHER & HIS KITE.

Designed expressly for the Columbian Magazine by J.L. Morton

Franklin and son William fly a kite during a lightning storm.
Illustration by J.L. Morton for the Columbian Magazine.

Be at War with your Vices, at

Peace with your
Neighbours,

and let every New-Year find you

a better Man.

—*POOR RICHARD IMPROVED* (1755)

Our new Constitution is now
established, and has an appearance

that promises
permanency;

but in this world nothing
can be said to be certain, except

death and taxes.

—LETTER TO JEAN-BAPTISTE LEROY (NOVEMBER 13, 1789)

Remember that
time is
money.

—ADVICE TO A YOUNG TRADESMAN (1748)

*Benjamin Franklin's countenance on
the one-hundred-dollar bill, in closeup.*

Think of three Things,
whence you came,
where you are
going,
and to whom you must
account.

—*POOR RICHARD'S ALMANACK* (1755)

A photograph of Benjamin Franklin's print shop, produced between 1910 and 1920 from a glass negative.

Be in general
virtuous,
and you will
be happy.

—LETTER TO JOHN ALLEYNE (AUGUST 9, 1768)

What you would seem to be,

be really.

—*POOR RICHARD'S ALMANACK* (1744)

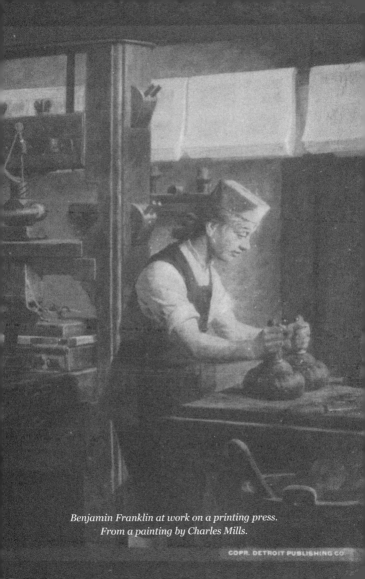

Benjamin Franklin at work on a printing press.
From a painting by Charles Mills.

About Cider Mill Press
Book Publishers

Good ideas ripen with time. From seed to harvest,
Cider Mill Press brings fine reading, information,
and entertainment together between the covers of
its creatively crafted books. Our Cider Mill bears
fruit twice a year, publishing a new crop of titles
each spring and fall.

Visit us on the web at
www.cidermillpress.com
or write to us at
12 Spring Street
PO Box 454
Kennebunkport, Maine 04046

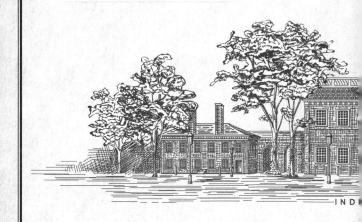

IND